Scary Creatures
HYENAS

Written by
John Malam

Created and designed
by David Salariya

Franklin Watts®
An Imprint of Scholastic Inc.
NEW YORK • TORONTO • LONDON • AUCKLAND • SYDNEY
MEXICO CITY • NEW DELHI • HONG KONG
DANBURY, CONNECTICUT

Author:

John Malam studied ancient history and archaeology at the University of Birmingham, England, after which he worked as an archaeologist at the Ironbridge Gorge Museum in Shropshire. He is now an author specializing in nonfiction books for children on a wide range of subjects. He lives in Cheshire with his wife and their two young children. Website: www.johnmalam.co.uk

Artists:
John Francis
Mark Bergin

Series Creator:

David Salariya was born in Dundee, Scotland. He established The Salariya Book Company in 1989. He has illustrated a wide range of books and has created many new series for publishers in the UK and overseas. He lives in Brighton, England, with his wife, illustrator Shirley Willis, and their son.

Editor: Stephen Haynes

Editorial Assistant: Rob Walker

Picture Research: Mark Bergin

Photo Credits:

t=top, b=bottom

Dreamstime: 22
Fotolia: 7, 8, 13, 14, 17, 21, 25
iStockphoto: 12, 18, 19t
NHPA: 19b

PAPER FROM
SUSTAINABLE
FORESTS

Created, designed, and produced by
The Salariya Book Company Ltd
25 Marlborough Place, Brighton BN1 1UB

A CIP catalog record for this title is available from the Library of Congress.

ISBN-13: 978-0-531-21746-7 (Lib. Bdg.)
978-0-531-21900-3 (Pbk.)
ISBN-10: 0-531-21746-9 (Lib. Bdg.)
0-531-21900-3 (Pbk.)

Published in 2009 in the United States by
Franklin Watts
An Imprint of Scholastic Inc.
557 Broadway
New York, NY 10012

Printed in China

Contents

Spotted hyenas

Zebras

What Are Hyenas?

Hyenas look like dogs, but are not closely related to them. They are fierce **carnivores** that hunt and **scavenge** food, mainly at night. Spotted, brown, and striped hyenas live in groups. The aardwolf lives on its own.

There are four different **species** of hyena. Each species can be recognized by the pattern and length of its fur. The spotted hyena is the biggest species. The aardwolf is the smallest.

X-Ray Vision

Hold the next page up to the light to see the skeleton of a spotted hyena.

See what's inside

Spotted hyena

Brown hyena

Aardwolf

Striped hyena

Hyenas live in **savanna** (dry grassland) regions of Africa. The small maps of Africa show where each species lives. The striped hyena is also found in the Middle East and Asia.

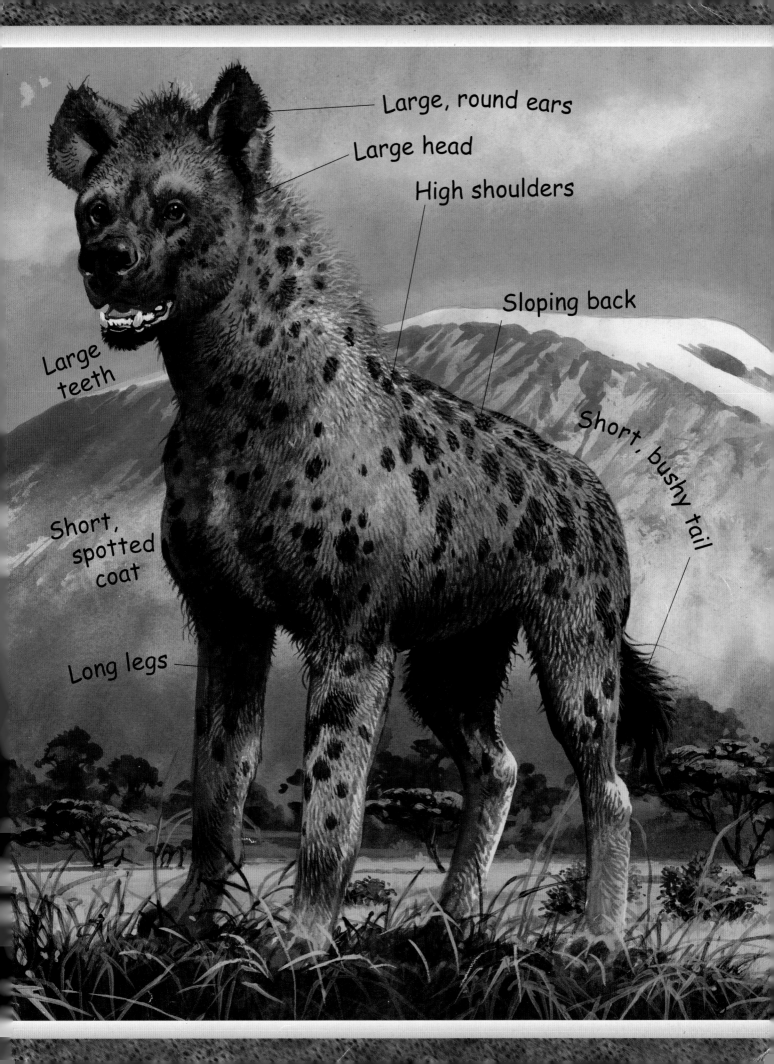

Large, round ears

Large head

High shoulders

Sloping back

Large teeth

Short, bushy tail

Short, spotted coat

Long legs

Large skull

Strong jaws with
32–34 teeth

4 toes

What Do Hyenas Eat?

The main food of hyenas is meat. Some hyenas also eat fruit and vegetables, which give them moisture when water is scarce. Hyenas are **predators**. They hunt beetles, birds, hares, grasshoppers, and termites. They will also tackle larger **mammals** such as gazelles, warthogs, wildebeests, and zebras. Hyenas are also **scavengers**. They eat meat from the **carcasses** of animals killed by other predators. Aardwolves eat mostly termites.

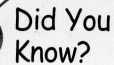

Did You Know?

The only parts of an animal that a hyena cannot digest completely are the hair, hooves, and horns. It swallows these, then coughs them up in a big **hairball**.

This is a spotted hyena. It eats more meat than any other hyena species. It rarely eats fruit or vegetables. Like the brown and the striped hyena, the spotted hyena makes food **caches**. These are stores of meat hidden away in grassy thickets, and even underwater. The hyena visits its stores when it is hungry.

How Do Hyenas Find Food in the Dark?

Hyenas are active at night. They have an excellent sense of smell and sniff the air for signs of **carrion** (rotting meat). Their hearing is also very good, and they listen for **prey** moving in the dark.

Did You Know?

Hyenas have better hearing than humans. They hear hyena calls that human ears cannot pick up. The calls let hyenas know where a carcass or other food has been found.

Spotted hyenas **forage** for food mainly in the low light of dusk and dawn. When they are scavenging, they use their keen senses of sight and smell to find carrion.

Spotted hyena

Water buffalo carcass

Spotted hyena cub

The spotted hyena is the only species that is active in the day as well as at night. All hyenas have good vision at night and in poor light. They have a special layer (called the **tapetum**) at the back of their eyes that magnifies light. In between their daily foraging times, hyenas are at rest.

How Do Hyenas Kill Their Prey?

A pair of spotted hyenas approach a herd of zebras.

The zebras do not sense any danger because the hyenas are walking slowly, not rushing toward them.

Hyenas are skillful hunters. They work alone or in pairs or groups, searching for an animal to attack. Spotted hyenas will single out a prey animal from a group of animals. One hyena walks quickly up to the group, then breaks into a run. The group scatters, and the strongest animals escape. The young and weak are left behind, and the hyena chooses one to kill.

Spotted hyena

Hunting a zebra

An adult zebra will feed about twelve hyenas. They eat quickly, climbing over the carcass and wriggling under each other to get at it. The only part they will not touch is the rumen (part of the stomach). The zebra is eaten in about thirty minutes—bones and all!

When they are very close to the herd, the hyenas start to run. They single out a zebra and chase it. Other hyenas join in. The zebra soon becomes tired and slows down, and then the hyenas come right up to it.

Zebra

Did You Know?

A hyena kills small prey by biting it around the neck or back, then shaking it until it is dead. This method of killing is known as a **death shake**.

They bite at the zebra's legs and pull its tail. The zebra falls to the ground, and the hyenas surround it. They bite into its soft belly, and within a few minutes the zebra is dead.

Do Hyenas Laugh?

Not really. The spotted hyena is one of Africa's noisiest animals. It has about eleven different calls, and one of them sounds like a giggle or a laugh. That's why its nickname is the "laughing hyena." It isn't really laughing— just making a noise that sounds like a laugh to us.

Spotted hyena "laughing"

Whoops, giggles, yells, growls, grunts, groans, barks, whines, screams, and squeals are some of the many noises made by spotted, brown, and striped hyenas. The aardwolf is the quietest member of the hyena family. It calls out only when it gets into a fight.

Young hyenas make squealing noises, which they can keep up for several minutes at a time. The squeals have two meanings. They can be either a greeting call or a begging-for-food call. They are always made to an adult.

How Do Hyenas Say Hello?

When two hyenas meet, they sniff each other's mouth, head, and neck. Then they sniff the sides of their bodies and their bottoms. This is a hyena greeting ceremony.

X-Ray Vision

Hold the next page up to the light to see what's inside the spotted hyena.

ee what's inside

Spotted hyena cubs sniffing each other

Why do hyenas sniff?

Sniffing is a way of getting to know each other. Every hyena has its own smell which members of its group learn to recognize.

Even if they have been apart for only a few minutes, hyenas still greet each other by sniffing. The more junior (less important) hyena usually sniffs first. The senior (more important) hyena often yawns while it is being sniffed.

Spotted hyenas greeting

A spotted hyena usually gives birth to two cubs. Aardwolves, brown hyenas, and striped hyenas usually have three or four cubs. Mothers carry their babies for about three to four months before giving birth to them.

Twin cubs in the mother's body

Where Do Baby Hyenas Live?

Baby hyenas live in a **den**. The den may be a hole in the ground or it may be in a cave. The cubs' mother comes to the den several times a day to **suckle** them. After a few weeks, the cubs are ready to venture outside the den.

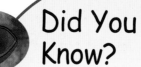

Did You Know?

After a number of months, the hyena mother stops suckling her cubs. The cubs don't like this! They throw a **weaning** tantrum, circling their mother and whining.

A spotted hyena and her cubs. The mother raises the cubs by herself—the father has nothing to do with them.

Many cubs from different mothers live in the same den. It's messy, with food scraps and hairballs all over the place.

What Is a Hyena Clan?

Most hyenas live in family groups, or **clans**. There can be as many as 100 or as few as ten in a clan. Each clan has its own territory. Adults **scent mark** the edges of their clan territory with an oily paste. They rub it onto grass stems. The scent warns hyenas from other clans to keep out.

Did You Know?

Hyenas mark the edges of their territory with urine and dung. It's another way of scent marking the boundaries. These "toilet" areas are shared with the next clan.

A hyena family group

Did You Know?

Fresh hyena dung is green. When it dries out it turns white because it contains so much calcium from the bones eaten by the hyena.

As a hyena walks along the edge of its clan territory, it rubs spots of scent onto the grass. It smells like soap. Human noses can detect a hyena scent mark for about 30 days. A hyena can probably smell it for longer.

Clan territories can cover very large areas. Hyenas always defend their ground from strangers. If a hyena enters a neighboring territory, a fight usually breaks out. A resident hyena runs up to the stranger and bites and pulls at its neck. The stranger doesn't bite back. It gives in and goes home.

Do Hyenas Have Enemies?

Spotted hyenas have one natural enemy—the lion. Hyenas and lions prey on the same large mammals. They both hunt zebras and various species of antelope, such as wildebeests, topi, gazelles, and impala. Competing for the same food can lead to fights, especially when hyenas try to rob lions of their kills.

Did You Know?

Spotted hyenas take food left by lions right away. Brown hyenas are not so brave—they keep their distance and wait about half an hour before taking the food.

Spotted hyenas approach a feeding lion. They walk shoulder to shoulder, which is a sign that they are on the attack. They are not afraid of the lion.

They try to frighten the lion away with growls and grunts. When it runs off, the hyenas move in and steal its kill.

Lions, like hyenas, would rather scavenge a free meal than spend time and energy in hunting one down.

The noisy calls of hyenas attract lions. If they find hyenas feeding, the lions will try to take the food from them.

Did You Know?

Lion mothers leave their cubs for many hours at a time. The cubs try to stay hidden, but if a hyena finds them it will grab one, take it away, and eat it.

How Fast Can a Hyena Run?

Hyenas have three speeds: walking, trotting, and running. Their walking speed is about 1 to 2.5 miles per hour (2 to 4 kph), and trotting is about 5 mph (8 kph). They can run as fast as 37 mph (60 kph). Hyenas can keep up their top speed only for short bursts before they get tired and have to slow down.

Did You Know?

The spotted hyena can keep up a steady speed of 30 mph (50 kph) over many miles before catching its prey or giving up the chase.

Trotting along at the edge of a lake, this spotted hyena is hoping to catch a flamingo. When it trots, a hyena has a long, ambling stride.

Spotted hyenas running

When a hyena runs fast, the lower parts of its legs appear to be loose-jointed. This is especially true of its back legs, which flop out to the side.

How far do hyenas travel?

In the search for food, the brown hyena travels the farthest. Every night it covers about 19 miles (31 km). The spotted hyena covers about 16 miles (26 km), and the striped hyena 12.5 miles (20 km).

Did You Know?

The wildebeest (a kind of antelope) has a top speed of about 50 mph (80 kph). That's faster than a hyena—but the wildebeest tires sooner than the hyena, so it eventually gets caught by the chasing predator.

Are Hyenas Endangered?

Many African mammals are **endangered**. They are at risk because their **habitats** are being destroyed, and because **poachers** hunt them. Hyenas are not likely to die out because there are many of them in the wild. However, they do face some threats to their lives.

Spotter plane

The brown hyena is the rarest species of hyena. Because it sometimes attacks farm animals, farmers shoot it, poison it, and trap it with snares. Even though only one **rogue** hyena might be responsible for the killing, some farmers believe every brown hyena is a danger to their livestock.

The Brown Hyena Research Project in Namibia studies brown hyenas. Radio collars have been fitted to hyenas from different clans.

Radio receiver

Radio transmitter

The collars send out signals that allow the hyenas' movements to be tracked by scientists on the ground or in the air.

All hyenas are at risk from road vehicles. Every year many are run over by cars and trucks. In Namibia, road signs (right) warn drivers if they are crossing hyena territory. The signs remind them to watch out for hyenas wandering onto the road.

Hyenas are also at risk from hunters, who shoot them for fun. In Cameroon, Senegal, and Côte d'Ivoire they are killed for meat. In Burkina Faso, Mozambique, and Tanzania some hyena body parts are used in traditional medicines.

In areas where locusts are a problem, poison is sprayed from planes. The poison can fall on hyenas and kill them as well as the locusts.

Brown hyena

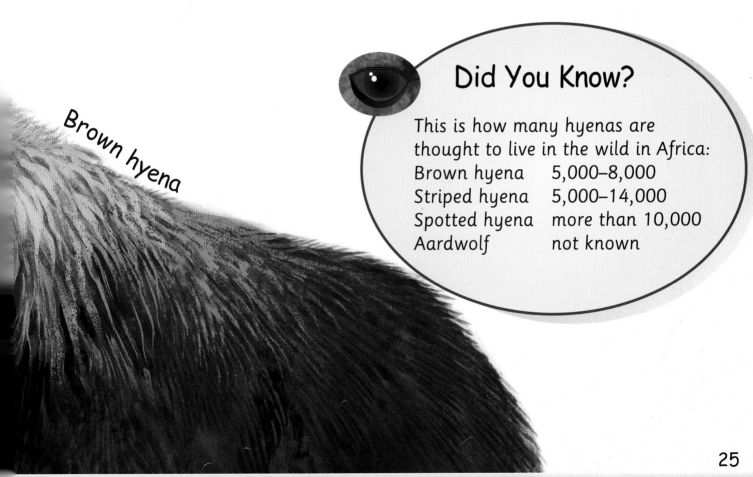

Did You Know?

This is how many hyenas are thought to live in the wild in Africa:

Brown hyena	5,000–8,000
Striped hyena	5,000–14,000
Spotted hyena	more than 10,000
Aardwolf	not known

Who Thinks Hyenas Are Scary?

Traditional stories from Africa link hyenas with witches and bad luck. They're like some of the stories told about cats in Europe and North America. African **folktales** describe how witches turn into hyenas—so perhaps

it's not surprising that some people find hyenas scary. Even though these are only made-up stories, people can be very superstitious about hyenas (and cats!).

In Sudan, in north Africa, a folktale describes hyenas as shape-shifters—part human, part animal. They are "were-hyenas" that attack people at night.

Did You Know?

In Africa, some people believe that hyena whiskers, tails, and ears have magical healing properties. They are used in traditional African medicines.

A folktale from the east African country of Tanzania claims that every witch has a hyena. According to this story, the witches ride their hyenas at night into the forest, where they gather together to boast about all the evil things they have done.

Hyena and Hare
A Folktale from East Africa

Once upon a time, Hyena and Hare were hungry. They were so hungry they went to a village and offered to do a farmer's gardening in return for food. The farmer accepted their help, and gave them a pot of beans. It was enough to feed them both for one day.

Hyena and Hare made a fire. They poured water over the beans, put the pot on the fire, and then left it to boil while they got on with their work in the farmer's garden.

Hyena's skin

By midday, the air was filled with the tasty smell of cooked beans. It was time to eat. Hyena said he needed to wash, and ran to a nearby stream. As soon as he was out of sight, he slipped off his skin, turned into a monster, and ran back. Hare got a terrible shock and fled, leaving all the beans for Hyena to eat.

After he had eaten, Hyena got dressed again in his own skin. When Hare came back, he found Hyena standing over the empty pot. Hare tried to explain what had happened, but Hyena accused Hare of eating the beans!

Hare tried to be brave. He said that if the beast came back the next day, he would shoot it with an arrow. Hyena took Hare's bow and scratched away some of the wood to make it weak.

The next day, the hyena-beast appeared again. Hare took aim, but the bow snapped where Hyena had weakened it. Hare ran for his life, and Hyena ate all the beans. Hare went hungry again.

By now, Hare was becoming suspicious. On the third day, he made a new bow and hid it in the grass. He said nothing to Hyena.

Sure enough, the hyena-beast came, but Hare was ready and shot it dead. He then saw that the "monster" had been Hyena all along. As he ate his first meal in days, Hare remembered the saying: "Greed does not pay."

Hyena Facts

Spotted, brown, and striped hyenas have bone-crushing teeth. Their bite is so powerful, they can break open bones as chunky as the thigh bone of a giraffe.

The spotted hyena is the tallest and heaviest hyena. It's about the size of a wolf. Females are about 34 inches (86 cm) high and weigh about 150 pounds (70 kg). Males are slightly smaller.

The aardwolf is the smallest hyena, about the size of a fox. Males and females are about 17 inches (45 cm) high and weigh about 22 pounds (10 kg).

Hyenas may look like dogs, but their closest living relatives are mongooses.

Brown hyenas catch and eat seal pups along the coast of Namibia in southern Africa.

Hyenas do not make good pets. In Nigeria, west Africa, baby spotted hyenas are taken from their parents and kept as pets by people who want them as status symbols. When they become adults, these captive hyenas are sometimes killed because they are too difficult to take care of.

Hyenas live for about twelve years in the wild.

A sleeping hyena curls up like a dog and puts its muzzle on its paws.

In ancient times, dried white hyena dung was crushed to make a powder called *album graecum* ("Greek white"). It was used in medicine and as a face powder.

The aardwolf tries to make itself appear bigger than it really is by raising its shaggy mane and tail.

When a hyena wants to show that it is of lower status (junior) to another member of its clan, it crawls on its paws. It makes itself appear smaller than the hyena it is trying to please.

In the town of Harar, Ethiopia, people put food out for spotted hyenas.

The Banda people of central Africa call the spotted hyena a *bongo*. To the Nyanja of Zambia it's a *fisi*, while the Gouragi of Ethiopia know it as a *woraba*.

Glossary

cache A hidden store of food.

carcass The body of a dead animal.

carnivore An animal that eats mostly meat.

carrion Dead and rotting flesh.

clan A large group of related animals.

death shake A way of shaking an animal with enough force to kill it.

den The place where a group of animals lives or meets.

endangered Likely to die out.

folktale A traditional story that has been told for many years.

forage To go out looking for food.

habitat The place in the wild in which an animal usually lives.

hairball A mass of hair and undigested body parts coughed up by a predator.

mammal A warm-blooded animal that feeds its young on mother's milk.

poacher A person who kills animals illegally.

predator An animal that hunts another animals for food.

prey An animal that is killed and eaten by a predator.

rogue An animal that has left its herd or pack and lives and hunts by itself.

savanna (or **savannah**) A habitat consisting of grassland that is dry for part of the year and has some trees or bushes.

scavenge To search for and eat dead meat and food scraps left by other animals.

scavenger An animal that scavenges.

scent mark A smelly patch left by an animal to mark its territory.

species A group of animals or plants that look alike, live in the same way, and produce young that do the same.

suckle To feed babies on mother's milk.

tapetum A reflecting layer at the back of the eye of certain animals that helps them to see in low light.

weaning Teaching young mammals to eat solid food instead of mother's milk.

31

Index